FARMS AND VILLAGES

by

Joanna Brundle

©2017
Book Life
King's Lynn
Norfolk PE30 4LS

ISBN: 978-1-78637-059-4

Written by:
Joanna Brundle

Edited by:
Grace Jones

Designed by:
Natalie Carr

FARMS AND VILLAGES

Contents......

Look for the words in **bold** in the Glossary on page 23.

YOUR **LOCAL** AREA

What is a **Farm?**

A farm is an area of land, used for growing **crops** or raising animals. Farms can be very small, with just enough land for a farmer to feed his or her family. Some farms cover huge areas and produce enough food to feed thousands of people.

A small farm in South Africa

Did you know? The three biggest food crops in the world are wheat, maize and rice.

Combine harvesters cut through a giant wheat field.

Farms that grow crops, like wheat and barley, are called arable farms. Pastoral farms raise animals for their meat and sometimes wool. Farms that grow crops and raise animals are called mixed farms.

Farms that keep cows for their milk are called dairy farms.

A mixed farm

Farms that do not use any **chemicals** are called organic farms.

What is a Village?

A village is a **rural settlement**, which is larger than a **hamlet**, but smaller than a town. Villages are made up of groups of houses and other buildings, like a church and sometimes a shop or school.

Most villages have open, public spaces. It may be a grassy village green or a square, where villagers can meet to hold local **festivals** and to buy and sell their goods at farmers' markets.

In Australia, a village is called a township. The term "village" is used for a shopping or **tourist** area.

A village square in Austria

A food market in the village of Kanha, India

Where and Why?

Farms have developed where the soil, weather and **landscape** are suitable for growing crops or raising animals. In order to grow well, most crops need warm summers and **fertile** soil that is not too wet. Cool summers and high rainfall help grass to grow, which then provides food for sheep, cattle and goats.

A stony hillside is suitable for animals, but not for growing crops.

Maize needs plenty of sun to ripen.

People and animals need water to survive, so many villages were built near to streams and rivers, often where the water could be crossed easily. Villages also grew because people needed to come together to buy and sell their animals and crops.

Fishing villages like this one in Vietnam have developed along the coast.

Farms and Villages in the Past

Farming used to provide jobs for many people. Work was done by hand and **ploughs** were pulled by horses. At harvest time, everyone helped to harvest the crops.

Nowadays, crop sprayers like this or light aircraft called crop dusters spray chemicals to kill pests.

A milking shed, like this one, is called a parlour.

Horse manure was good for the soil but there were no chemicals to kill weeds and pests.

Milking used to be done by hand but nowadays machines have replaced humans.

Most villagers worked on farms but some villages, known as pit villages, grew up where there were local **resources** like coal or tin to be mined. A lack of transport meant that most people stayed near their villages all of their lives.

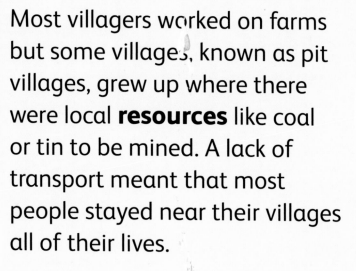

pelen rooien.

Before the invention of trains and motor cars in the 1800's, people had to walk or use horses to get about.

These villagers are digging potatoes by hand.

What is it Like to Live in the Countryside?

People who live in the countryside can enjoy fresh air, open spaces and outdoor activities, like walking and bird watching. Houses usually have gardens or land around them and people might keep animals such as horses or chickens.

An Australian Eastern Spinebill perches on a bottle brush plant.

What season of the year do you think it is?

A family enjoying a walk in the forest.

Living in the countryside can be difficult too. There is little public transport and people often have to travel farther to services like schools and banks. In some villages, people who have bought holiday homes have made houses too expensive for local people.

Villages may be cut off by heavy snow.

Villages usually have a smaller population than towns or cities.

Farm and Village Buildings

Farms usually have a farmhouse, where a farmer lives with his or her family. Barns provide shelter for animals and storage for machines, like tractors. Dutch barns, which are common in the UK, have a roof but no sides and are used for storing hay and straw.

A Dutch barn

Wheat and barley are stored in metal grain silos, like these.

Village homes are often built from local stone or other local resources and usually have gardens. Most villages have a church.

Can you see how the stones have been fitted together to make the wall?

A stone cottage in Wales

A village store in Western Australia

The village shop may also be the post office, petrol station and café all rolled into one!

Village Life Around the World

Many people who live in villages around the world provide everything they need for themselves. They grow their own food and build their homes from local resources.

Villagers in India carrying home water from the well

This house in Kenya is made of wood, bamboo, mud and cow dung!

Many villages have no electricity or running water.

Children harvesting rice in Thailand

Many villages have only a basic school like this open-air one in India.

Some children are not able to go to school at all because they have to help their families by working in the fields.

17

Sheep Farming in Australia

Farms cover almost two thirds of Australia's land and include large areas of grassland for sheep farms, called sheep stations. The most common sheep is the merino, which gives fine but strong wool.

Removing the wool, or fleece, from an animal is called shearing.

An Australian merino sheep

A sheep shearer in Queensland, Australia

Sheep stations are usually far away from other settlements so some have a runway for light aircraft to bring supplies. The Royal Flying Doctor Service comes to station workers who are ill.

An Australian kelpie, used for rounding up sheep

A Royal Flying Doctor Service plane

Station workers ride horses to herd the sheep.

19

Farms and Villages in the Future

The temperature on planet Earth is slowly increasing. Higher temperatures may cause damage to crops and the environment. Melting snow and ice may cause sea levels to rise and flood farmland.

Scientists are looking at natural ways of dealing with pests, like introducing lady-birds to eat **aphids**.

You can help to reduce global warming by using less energy.

Crops damaged by heat

Scientists are developing GM or genetically modified crops, which have fewer **pests** and a bigger **yield**.

Farmers can receive extra money for doing things that help wildlife, like planting hedgerows.

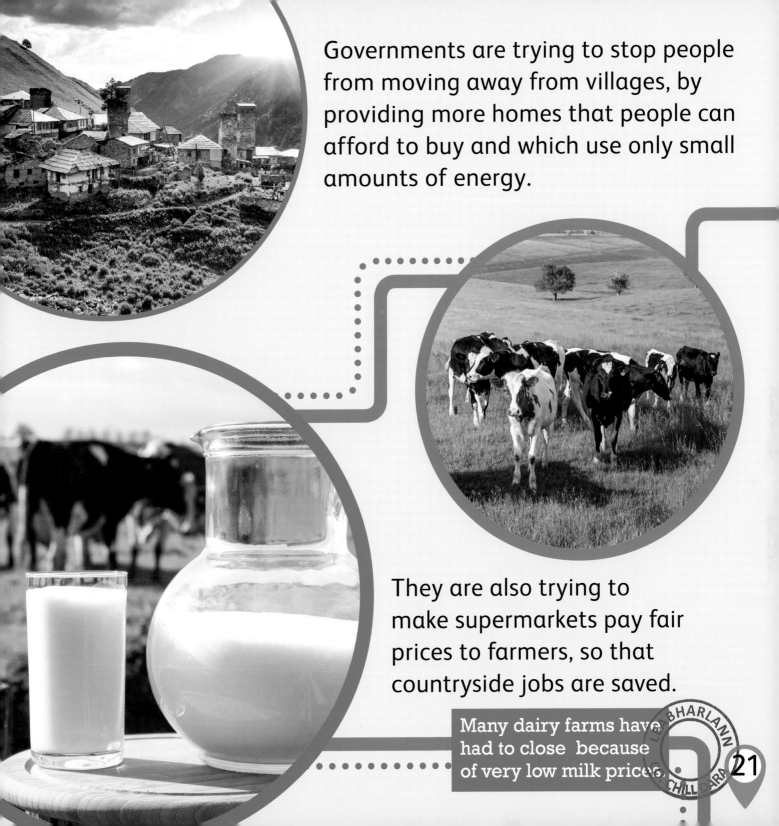

Governments are trying to stop people from moving away from villages, by providing more homes that people can afford to buy and which use only small amounts of energy.

They are also trying to make supermarkets pay fair prices to farmers, so that countryside jobs are saved.

Many dairy farms have had to close because of very low milk prices.

Wildlife

Farms and villages are full of wildlife, like bees, butterflies, squirrels, deer and owls. Next time you are in the countryside, why not try making a simple tally chart to count the insects, wild flowers or birds you see.

A swallowtail butterfly and a bee feeding on a sunflower

Harvest mouse in a cornfield

Glossary

aphids   small insects that feed by sucking the juices of a plant

chemicals   substances produced naturally or by scientists, for example weed killers

crops   plants grown because they are useful, usually as food

fertile   having rich soil which can grow crops

festivals   times when people come together to celebrate special events or times of year

hamlet   a very small group of houses, smaller than a village and with no church

landscape   a stretch of land, showing features such as hills and valleys

ploughs   large pieces of farming equipment, used for turning over the soil, ready for planting

resources   useful things

rural   to do with the countryside

settlements   places people live permanently, like villages or towns

tourists   people who visit other places for enjoyment

yield   the amount produced

Index

A
animals 4–5, 8–9, 14

B
barley 5, 14
barns 14

C
chickens 12
churches 6, 15
countryside 12–13, 22
crops 4–5, 8–10, 20

D
dairy farms 5, 21

F
food 4, 7, 16

H
horses 10–12, 19

S
schools 6, 13, 17
sheep 8, 18–19
shopping 7
shops 6, 15
soil 8, 100

T
tractors 14
transport 11, 13

W
water 9, 16
weather 8, 20
wheat 4–5, 14
wildlife 20, 22
wool 5, 18

Photo Credits

Photocredits: Abbreviations: l–left, r–right, b–bottom, t–top, c–centre, m–middle.
Front Cover tl – Creative Travel Projects, m – JeniFoto. tr – Simun Ascic. b – Polarpx. 2 – kwest. 3 – FamVeld. 4mr – EcoPrint. 4bl – Todd Klassy. 5tr – Pixeljoy. 5bl – David Steele. 6 – FamVeld. 7br – SJ Travel Photo and Video. 7bl – cornfield.8tl – Photo Image. 8b – CREATISTA. 9 – Hang Dinh. 10mr – Fotokostic. 10bl – Evgeny Sribnyjj. 11tr – Patryk Kosmider. 11bl – Patricia Hofmeester. 12bl – Tatiana Chekryzhova. 12br – DuxX.13tr – Maksim Vivtsaruk. 13br– Elena Elisseeva. 14mr – Ruud Morijn Photographer. 14bl – Nikifor Todorov. 15tr - Radek Sturgolewski. 15bl - David Steele. 16mr – FiledIMAGE. 16bl – Dr Ajay Kumar Singh. 17tl – thiraphonthongaram. 17br – Amlan Mathur. 18mr – ChameleonsEye. 18bl – John Carnemolla. 19tr – K.A.Willis. 19bl – VanderWolf Images. 20mr – sorayut. 20bl – Dimijana. 21tl – Creative Travel Projects. 21mr – Todd Klassy. 21bl – aquariagirl1970. 22b – Paul Tymon. 22r – Betty Shelton. Images are courtesy of Shutterstock.com. With thanks to Getty Images, Thinkstock Photo and iStockphoto.